W9-AVN-367

Joseph Priestley House

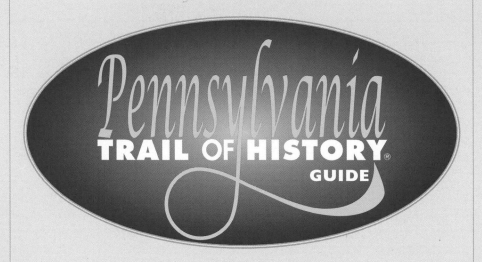

Text by Alison Duncan Hirsch
Photographs by Kyle R. Weaver

STACKPOLE BOOKS

PENNSYLVANIA HISTORICAL
AND MUSEUM COMMISSION

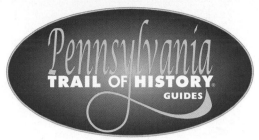

Kyle R. Weaver, Series Editor
Tracy Patterson, Designer

Published by
STACKPOLE BOOKS
5067 Ritter Road
Mechanicsburg, Pennsylvania 17055

Copyright © 2003 by Stackpole Books. All rights reserved, including the right to reproduce this book or portions thereof in any form or by any means, electronic or mechanical, including photocopying, recording, or by any information storage and retrieval system, without permission in writing from the publisher. All inquiries should be addressed to Stackpole Books.

Pennsylvania Trail of History® is a registered trademark of the Pennsylvania Historical and Museum Commission.

Printed in the United States of America
2 4 6 8 10 9 7 5 3 1
FIRST EDITION

Maps by Caroline Stover

Photography
Kyle R. Weaver: 3, 5, 24, 32, 33, 36–47
Joseph Priestley House staff photographer: cover

Library of Congress Cataloging-in-Publication Data

Hirsch, Alison Duncan.
    Joseph Priestley House : Pennsylvania trail of history guide / text by Alison Duncan Hirsch ; photographs by Kyle R. Weaver.—1st ed.
        p. cm.—(Pennsylvania trail of history guides)
    Includes bibliographical references.
    ISBN 0–8117–2629–0 (pbk.)
    1. Priestley, Joseph, 1733–1804. 2. Chemists—Great Britain—Biography. 3. Priestley, Joseph, 1733–1804—Homes and haunts—Pennsylvania—Northumberland—Guidebooks. 4. Northumberland (Pa.)—Guidebooks. I. Title. II. Series.

QD22.P8 H55 2003
540'.92—dc21

2002012230

Contents

Editor's Preface

The fruits of immigration in Pennsylvania are evident in the cultural, industrial, and economic contributions made by the groups that settled in the state throughout its history. Perhaps the most remarkable individual who immigrated to Pennsylvania was the Englishman who discovered oxygen and whose political writings advanced the cause of free expression throughout the Western world—Joseph Priestley. Today, Priestley's house in Northumberland is preserved by the Pennsylvania Historical and Museum Commission (PHMC). Stackpole Books is proud to join with the PHMC in featuring the site in this volume of the Pennsylvania Trail of History Guides, a series on the museums and historic sites administered by the PHMC.

The series was conceived and created by Stackpole Books with the cooperation of the PHMC's Division of Publications and Bureau of Historic Sites and Museums. Donna Williams heads the latter, and she and her staff of professionals review the text of each guidebook for accuracy and have made many valuable recommendations. Diane Reed, Chief of Publications, has facilitated relations between the PHMC and Stackpole from the project's inception, organized the review process with the commission, and attended to numerous details related to the venture.

For this volume, Andrea Bashore, the Administrator of the Joseph Priestley House, went out of her way to ensure that all the necessary resources were available to us. She guided us through the site and archives, put us in touch with the appropriate contacts at other related institutions, and provided us with constructive criticism in the editorial stage of the project. Brooke Dearman, Custodial Guide, was helpful in preparing each of the rooms for photography, including the daunting task of removing archival covers from all of the books in Priestley's Library.

Alison Duncan Hirsch, the author of the text, has a Ph.D. in history from Columbia University and has taught history and American studies at Penn State University and Dickinson College. She has written numerous articles on early Pennsylvania history and coedited several volumes of *The Papers of William Penn* and *The Diary of Elizabeth Drinker*. Here she presents a brief biography of Priestley, recounts his later years in Northumberland, and guides the reader on a tour of the house and laboratory of Pennsylvania's most famous immigrant.

Kyle R. Weaver, Editor
Stackpole Books

Introduction to the Site

The Joseph Priestley House, in Northumberland, Pennsylvania, was the American home of the scientist-clergyman-teacher, who is best known as the man who discovered oxygen. Joseph Priestley lived in the house with his family from 1798 until his death in 1804. A central figure in the Anglo-American Enlightenment, Priestley lived most of his life in England, where he became an outspoken proponent of Unitarianism, freedom of religion, and the American and French Revolutions. He and his wife, Mary, immigrated to the newly formed United States in 1794 in search of religious and political freedom, as well as the financial freedom to pursue his scientific interests.

Under construction for nearly four years, Priestley's rural Georgian manor on the Susquehanna River housed perhaps the finest American laboratory and private library of its day. The house provides visitors with a window into not only his life, but also the lives of women, children, and servants in early rural Pennsylvania. Administered today by the Pennsylvania Historical and Museum Commission, the site is a National Historic Landmark and a National Historic Chemical Landmark.

13 POND BUILDING

The idea for a Priestley museum originated in the early twentieth century with Dr. George Gilbert Pond, professor of chemistry and dean of the School of Natural Sciences at Pennsylvania State College, now Penn State University. Pond purchased the property at auction in 1919. After his death the following year, college trustees took over management of the site and in 1926 erected this building in his memory. That year, when the American Chemical Society met in Philadelphia, a delegation came by chartered train to the Priestley site for the dedication of the new building. Initially designed as a fireproof museum for Priestley's books and scientific apparatus, it was used for a while as the site's visitor center, until the present Visitor Center was built. It is presently closed to the public, but the PHMC hopes to renovate it as an exhibition and public program space.

For more information on hours, tours, programs, and activities at the Joseph Priestley House, visit **www.phmc.state.pa.us** or call **570-473-9474**.

47

Further Reading

Clark, John Ruskin. *Joseph Priestley: "A Comet in the System."* San Diego: Torch Publications, 1990.

Graham, Jenny. *Revolutionary in Exile: The Emigration of Joseph Priestley to America, 1794–1804.* Philadelphia: American Philosophical Society, 1995.

Hiebert, Erwin N., Aaron J. Ihde, and Robert E. Schofield. *Joseph Priestley: Scientist, Theologian, and Metaphysician.* Edited by Lester Kieft and Bennett R. Willeford. Lewisburg, Pa.: Bucknell University Press, 1980.

Holt, Ann. *A Life of Joseph Priestley.* Westport, Conn.: Greenwood Press, 1970.

Lukehart, Peter, ed. *Joseph Priestley in America, 1794–1804.* Carlisle, Pa.: Trout Gallery, Dickinson College, 1994.

Park, Mary Cathryne. "Joseph Priestley and the Problem of Pantisocracy," *Proceedings of the Delaware County Institute of Science* 11, no. 1 (1947).

Priestley, Joseph. *Autobiography of Joseph Priestley.* Introduction by Jack Lindsay. Teaneck, N.J.: Fairleigh Dickinson University Press, 1970.

———. *Joseph Priestley: Selections from His Writings.* State College, Pa.: Himes Printing, 1962.

———. *Political Writings.* Edited by Peter Miller. Cambridge, Mass.: Cambridge University, 1993.

Robbins, Caroline. "Honest Heretic: Joseph Priestley in America, 1794–1804." *Proceedings of the American Philosophical Society* 106, no.1 (1962): 60–76.

Schofield, Robert. *The Enlightenment of Joseph Priestley: A Study of His Life and Work from 1733 to 1773.* University Park, Pa.: Pennsylvania State University Press, 1997.

———. *A Scientific Autobiography of Joseph Priestley (1733–1804).* Cambridge, Mass.: Massachusetts Institute of Technology Press, 1966.

On the Web
Chemical Heritage Foundation website: www.chemheritage.org

Also Available

**Anthracite Heritage Museum
and Scranton Iron Furnaces**

Brandywine Battlefield Park

Conrad Weiser Homestead

Cornwall Iron Furnace

Daniel Boone Homestead

Drake Well Museum and Park

Eckley Miners' Village

Ephrata Cloister

**Erie Maritime Museum and
U.S. Brig Niagara**

Hope Lodge and Mather Mill

Landis Valley Museum

Old Economy Village

Pennsbury Manor

Railroad Museum of Pennsylvania

*All titles are $10, plus shipping,
from Stackpole Books, 800-732-3669, www.stackpolebooks.com, or
The Pennsylvania Historical and Museum Commission, 800-747-7790,
www.phmc.state.pa.us*

Joseph Priestley and His World

In June 1794, an unusual immigrant arrived in Pennsylvania. Joseph Priestley (1733–1804), the discoverer of oxygen, was probably the most famous man to make a new home in America up until that time. From the moment he arrived, political and cultural leaders welcomed him and urged him to settle in one of the major cities of the new nation: Philadelphia, New York, or Boston. John Adams wrote to invite him to live in New England; Thomas Jefferson hoped he would settle in Virginia. But unlike other well-educated immigrants, who preferred to live in America's coastal urban centers, Priestley chose to live in a remote rural area of Pennsylvania. After their arrival in New York, he and his wife, Mary, continued on their journey until they reached the small town of Northumberland, in the central Susquehanna Valley. There Joseph and Mary Priestley began to plan for their new house.

Today Priestley is famous primarily as a scientist, but in his own lifetime, he was equally well known as a minister, theologian, teacher, author, and political thinker. In his mind, and in the minds of many of his contemporaries, these were not disconnected activities, but all aspects of "natural philosophy," or what we today would call "science." He published dozens of books on theology, history, science, education, and politics, always with the underlying, unifying themes of reason and the unfettered inquiry of knowledge. His dedication to freedom of thought eventually made him a dangerous man in the eyes of the English authorities, and their hostility was what drove him to immigrate with his family to America.

Above all, Joseph Priestley was a man who thought for himself. As a child, he learned the catechism of his family's Calvinist church, but early on he began to develop his own beliefs about religion. Foremost among his beliefs was the idea that religion should be rational and not contradict common sense or experimental knowledge. Eventually, after many years of study and thought, he came to be one of the founders of Unitarianism. He had come a long way from his Calvinist childhood.

Joseph Priestley, c. 1801. The renowned scientist, theologian, and political theorist was painted by Rembrandt Peale (1778–1860) near the end of his life. ARCHIVES AND SPECIAL COLLECTIONS, DICKINSON COLLEGE, CARLISLE, PENNSYLVANIA

FORMATIVE INFLUENCES

Joseph Priestley was born in a Yorkshire farmhouse, near the city of Leeds, England, on March 13, 1733. He was the first of six children born to Mary Swift and Jonas Priestley, whose profession was cloth-dressing, or scouring and pressing woolen cloth to thicken the woven material. According to family tradition, Joseph could recite his catechism by age four and was conducting scientific experiments by age eleven, when he sealed spiders in bottles to see how long they could survive in a closed environment.

When Joseph was seven, his mother died, and his father soon remarried. Joseph then went to live with a childless aunt and uncle, Sarah and John Keighley. His aunt taught him academic subjects at home and then sent him to a local school to learn Greek and Latin. He taught himself a system of shorthand invented by Peter Annet, a leading English freethinker. Young Joseph even sent Annet some suggestions for improving the system, along with a poem he had written, which Annet added to the revised edition of his book.

Joseph went on to study with a series of tutors. At age sixteen, he became ill, probably with tuberculosis, but he continued to teach himself. He learned math and algebra, as well as a multitude of languages: Hebrew, French, German, Dutch, Italian, Syrian, Chaldean, and Arabic. In 1752, he began university-level study at Daventry Academy. Since he was a dissenter—that is, not a member of the established Church of England—he could not have attended any of the leading universities, such as Oxford or Cambridge. Daventry was one of the best of the so-called dissenting academies that sprang up in England in the mid-eighteenth century, and Joseph Priestley received a good education there.

His aunt, a staunch Calvinist, regularly had dissenting ministers as guests, even when their theological opinions differed radically from her own. The varying opinions Joseph heard growing up led him to question the religious orthodoxies of his day. At age nineteen, when he applied for membership in his aunt's church in preparation for going into the ministry, his independent opinions caused problems for him. The church elders rejected him because he gave the wrong answers to questions about original sin; he could not bring himself to believe in the idea that "all the human race . . . were liable to the wrath of God, and the pains of hell for ever."

MINISTER, SCIENTIST, AND POLITICAL THEORIST

In spite of this setback of being rejected by his own family's congregation, Priestley later claimed that he "never lost sight of the great object of [his] studies, which was [to be] a Christian minister." Another obstacle he faced was a speech impediment, a hereditary stutter that he struggled with all his life. Upon graduation, he accepted a position as assistant minister at a church 150 miles from his home, in Needham Market, Suffolk, where his stutter, combined with his northern midlands accent, made his sermons difficult for the congregation to understand. In addition, his unorthodox beliefs soon got him into trouble; later, he admitted that he had been a "furious freethinker," which led to reductions in his salary and his aunt's refusal to continue to pay him an allowance. She did, however, pay for him to go to London for treatment of his stammer. The treatment was unsuccessful, but at least he had an opportunity to explore both Cambridge and London in his continuing program of self-education.

Priestley's tenure at Needham Market lasted just three years. His next position was much more suitable. Nantwich, in Cheshire, was much closer to home, and his new congregation found his sermons easier to understand and more to their liking. He was able to augment his income by opening a school, something he had tried unsuccessfully to do in Suffolk. In a small building next to his church, he taught thirty boys in one room, a handful of girls in another, six days a week. He began to develop his own teaching methods and tools: He wrote an English grammar textbook—one of the first of its kind—and purchased scientific equipment for the classroom. Soon the older students were "entertaining their parents and friends with experiments," and both Priestley and his school gained some fame. He had already begun to develop ideas about liberal arts education—ideas that after his move to the United States would earn him invitations to teach at the University of Virginia and Philadelphia College (later called the University of Pennsylvania).

By 1761, his reputation had earned him an invitation to teach at Warrington Academy, one of the most progressive of the new dissenting academies. He spent six "singularly happy" years there as the tutor in languages and literature, although he later admitted that he would have been more pleased with an appointment in natural philosophy. Still, he made the best of it and, among other endeavors, developed a series of lectures on constitutional history, which were later published in book form (1788). At Warrington, in May 1762, Priestley was finally ordained a minister by his fellow dissenting ministers. He was twenty-nine years old. A month later, he married eighteen-year-old Mary

CHRONOLOGY

1733 Priestley born at Birstal Fieldhead, Yorkshire, England, March 13

1742 Goes to live with aunt, Sarah Keighley

1752 Rejected for membership by Calvinist church; enters Daventry Academy

1755 Called to ministry at Needham Market Congregational Church, Suffolk

1758 Becomes minister at Nantwich, Cheshire

1761 Becomes tutor at Warrington Academy

1762 Marries Mary Wilkinson

1764 Receives LL.D. from Edinburgh University; founds fund for dissenting ministers' widows

1765 Publishes *Liberal Education for Civil and Active Life*

1766 Elected to the Royal Society

1767 Publishes *The History and Present State of Electricity, with Original Experiments*; invents method for making carbonated water; becomes minister at Mill Hill Chapel, Leeds

1768 Publishes *An Essay on the First Principles of Government; and on the Nature of Political, Civil, and Religious Liberty*

1769 Anonymously publishes *The Present State of Liberty in Great Britain and Her Colonies*

(continued)

9

Benjamin Franklin was rendered by Mason Chamberlain (1727–87) in London in 1762, a few years before Priestley's first meeting with the famous American diplomat-scientist. PHILADELPHIA MUSEUM OF ART (GIFT OF MR. AND MRS. WHARTON SINKLER)

Wilkinson, the only daughter of a well-to-do ironmaster. In 1764, he accepted the first of many honors that he was to receive: Edinburgh University conferred on him the degree of doctor of laws (LL.D.). From then on, he would be known as Dr. Priestley. That same year, he embarked on the first of several philanthropic ventures. Perhaps thinking of his own wife's security, he began a fund for the widows of dissenting ministers in Lancashire and Cheshire.

In 1765, Priestley began to write a history of scientific discoveries about electricity. He wrote that electricity was his "own favourite amusement," as it was for many in England, ever since the publication there of Benjamin Franklin's *New Experiments and Observations on Electricity.* Franklin himself was then in London, serving as Pennsylvania's representative at a time of growing turmoil in Britain's relations with its American colonies. (The colonies were then resisting the Stamp Act, and Franklin was in England trying to explain what Americans found so obnoxious about the new tax.) Priestley finagled an introduction to Franklin and, through him, met other men who had been performing electrical experiments. These men were all members of the Royal Society, the preeminent scientific association in England. They encouraged Priestley in his writing project and helped him find the necessary books. They also encouraged him to repeat the historic experiments for himself so that he could write from firsthand experience. His brother Timothy, a Calvinist minister much more orthodox than Joseph, agreed to help make the "electrifying machines," including a "kite of fine silk" that "was to bring electrical fire from the clouds," just as Franklin's kite had done.

While continuing his teaching at Warrington, Priestley conducted his experiments and wrote the history. His new scientific friends nominated him for membership in the Royal Society, and he was elected to the society in 1766. The following year, his first scientific book, *The History and Present State of Electricity, with Original Experiments,* came out to rave reviews from Europe's scientific community. It went through five English editions and was translated into French and German. Franklin purchased several copies for American institutions, including Harvard, Yale, and the American Philosophical Society in Philadelphia.

In spite of these honors and his general contentment with his situation, Priestley missed the ministry. He also knew that teaching alone was never going to make him financially successful, able to provide well for his wife and a growing family. (A daughter, Sarah, had been born in 1763.) In 1767, he accepted an invita-

tion to serve as minister of the New Meeting at Mill Hill Chapel in Leeds. This prestigious appointment must have given him some satisfaction, since it was so close to where, years earlier, he had been rejected for church membership. He already had a ready supply of sermons prepared, and he exchanged others freely with his friends in the ministry. In Leeds, for the first time since his own student days, he had plenty of time for thinking and writing.

Priestley spent five years as the minister at Mill Hill. During this time, his wife gave birth to two more children: Joseph Jr., born in 1768, and William, 1771. Priestley confined his teaching to his congregation. He taught the catechism to children, scripture to the intermediate level, and "natural and revealed religion" to young adults. To accompany each of these levels of instruction, he published books and a series of pamphlets on his religious ideas. He claimed to be presenting ideas that were common to all Christian churches, but religion was a contentious subject in the eighteenth century, and Priestley drew his share of criticism for his participation in the era's virulent pamphlet wars.

During the years in Leeds, Priestley continued his scientific work. In 1767, he began the experiments on air that would result in his most notable achievements. His house there was near a brewery, which provided opportunities for studying carbon dioxide, or "fixed air," as it was then called. He soon discovered a method for creating carbonated water, similar to naturally occurring mineral spa waters. His discovery would eventually give rise to today's worldwide soft drink industries. At this time, he began his practice of a yearly visit to London to meet with his publisher, to deliver papers at meetings of the Royal Society, and to renew friendships in per-

CHRONOLOGY

1770 Founds Leeds circulating library

1773 Becomes librarian and tutor for Lord Shelburne's family

1774 Announces his discovery of oxygen; tours Europe with Shelburne

1780 Leaves Shelburne's service; moves to Birmingham

1782 Publishes *History of the Corruptions of Christianity*

1785 Publishes *The Importance and Extent of Free Enquiry in Matters of Religion*

1786 Publishes *History of the Early Opinions Concerning Jesus Christ*; elected a member of American Philosophical Society

1791 Moves to London area after a mob destroys his Birmingham house, manuscripts, and equipment

1794 Immigrates to Pennsylvania; moves to Northumberland

1795 Writes final section of memoirs

1796 Wife, Mary, dies

1798 Moves into new house in Northumberland

1799 Discovers carbon monoxide

1801 Publishes *Letters to the Inhabitants of Northumberland and Its Neighbourhood*

1804 Dies at Northumberland

Minister at Leeds. *Despite his prominence as a scientist and political theorist, Priestley considered the ministry to be his primary vocation.* THE ROYAL SOCIETY, LONDON

son. Although he was a prolific letter writer and corresponded with scientists throughout Europe, there was no substitute for personal dialogue. In 1770, he helped found the first circulating library in Leeds, something Franklin had done in Philadelphia. Both men wanted to elevate the intellectual environment in which they lived, and their libraries survive today as testament to their success.

In Leeds, Priestley also made his entrance into the world of politics, first in coffeehouse discussions, and then in published works. The first of these was *An Essay on the First Principles of Government; and on the Nature of Political, Civil, and Religious Liberty*, published in 1768 in London and Dublin, and translated into Dutch in 1783. As a dissenter, Priestley was most concerned with the limitations nonconformists faced in a nation with an established state religion. He urged complete toleration for all, even Catholics—a radical idea for his

time, when Catholics were prohibited from voting or running for elected office in most of the Protestant world.

In 1769, Priestley entered the debate about the relationship between Britain and its American colonies with the publication of an anonymous pamphlet "by an Englishman," *The Present State of Liberty in Great Britain and Her Colonies*. Echoing ideas held at that time by Benjamin Franklin and many other Americans, who were not yet thinking about breaking from England, Priestley declared his intention "to make plain and intelligible, a just idea of natural and civil rights" owed to all British subjects, whichever side of the Atlantic they lived on. The oppressive taxation imposed on Americans had its counterparts in Parliamentary corruption and magistrates' attacks on basic liberties at home.

By the early 1770s, new opportunities were coming Priestley's way. He received an invitation to join Capt. James Cook's second voyage around the world as an astronomer, even though that was not his area of scientific expertise. Priestley accepted, with the stipulation that some provision be made for his family. Then, just as suddenly as it had come, the invitation was revoked. Priestley suspected that Oxford and Cambridge professor-clergymen had vetoed his appointment because of his unorthodox religious ideas, though it seems likely that his lack of experience in astronomy might have had more to do with the expedition's final choice of someone else.

Disappointment and the growing sense that he needed to provide better for his family's future led him to start thinking about America. But another opportunity arose first. William Petty, earl of Shelburne, a widower, was looking for a "gentleman of character and extensive knowledge and learning" to serve as a sort of intellectual companion and supervisor of his sons' education. After much indecision, Priestley accepted. In 1773, he took up his new post and thereby moved closer to both the physical and the social centers of power in the British world.

For the next seven years, Priestley's main job for Shelburne was to research various subjects being debated in Parliament, but this must not have taken up much of his time, for these were the most productive years in his scientific research. His laboratory at Bowood, Shelburne's Wiltshire estate, had more extensive equipment and space than he had ever enjoyed before. He lived most of the year with his family in a house in the neighboring village of Calne; during winters, he had an apartment at Lord Shelburne's residence in London. There he had more opportunity than ever to meet with fellow members of the Royal Society and the Whig Club, including Benjamin Franklin, with whom Priestley had many discussions about the conflict between Britain and the colonies. When the Revolution forced Franklin to leave England, he spent his last day there with Priestley. They read newspapers for the latest news from America, and Priestley remembered that "the tears trickled down [Franklin's] cheeks" as they read the news from Boston.

THE DISCOVERY OF OXYGEN
During his years working at Bowood, Priestley completed work on five of six volumes of his *Experiments and Observations*, in which he explained his discovery of oxygen, or what he called "dephlogisticated air," as well as other gases: ammonia, sulfur dioxide, nitrous oxide, and nitrogen dioxide. When he produced a gas by heating a sample of mercuric oxide, he discovered that in this new gas, candles burned

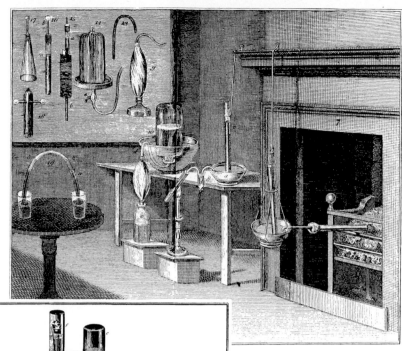

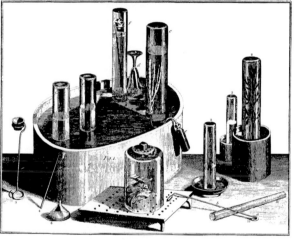

Experiments and Observations on Different Kinds of Air. *Priestley's monumental six-volume work on his discovery of oxygen and other gases includes these engravings of his laboratory and pneumatic chemistry apparatus.*

JOSEPH PRIESTLEY HOUSE

brighter and a mouse under glass could survive longer than with any other gas or air. When he himself breathed it in, his lungs "felt peculiarly light and easy for some time after," and he mused that this new gas might someday become a coveted luxury item. "I have discovered an air five or six times as good as common air," he wrote. At that time, scientists—including Priestley—did not understand air as a combination of gases, but rather spoke of different types of air. Priestley observed that green plants could restore air that had been depleted by animal respiration, an observation still relevant today in our concern for preserving balance in the earth's atmosphere and the global environment as a whole.

In 1774, Priestley accompanied Shelburne on a tour of Europe, and in Paris he met Continental scientists interested in his research. When the French scientist Antoine Lavoisier heard about Priestley's new "air," he recognized it as the missing piece of the puzzle he had been working on. Lavoisier then developed the modern

WHO REALLY DISCOVERED OXYGEN?

The eighteenth century was a heady time for discoveries about the natural world. When the century began, most European thinkers believed in the phlogiston theory, which held that when things burned, they emitted a volatile material (phlogiston) into the air. The air we breathe, which we now know is made up of a combination of gases, was thought to be one inseparable substance. There were no professional scientists at that time, but various people—teachers, doctors, apothecaries, wealthy hobbyists—began experimenting with the combustion process and eventually identified different types of "air": fixed air, or carbon dioxide; flammable air, or hydrogen; and noxious air, or nitrogen. But no one had yet identified the type of "air" necessary for animal and human life and for combustion.

Intrigued by the properties of different "airs," Joseph Priestley experimented with them, using an inverted container on a raised platform that could capture gases produced by various tests performed below it. On August 1, 1774, he conducted his most famous experiment. With a glass "burning lens," he focused sunlight on a lump of mercuric oxide. He called the gas he collected "dephlogisticated air."

Actually, more than a year earlier, Swedish apothecary Karl Wilhelm Scheele (1742–86) had independently isolated the same gas, which he called "fire air," by heating various substances together. But scientists in different countries had little means of communicating with each other, and Priestley and Scheele knew nothing about each other's work. Scheele did not publish his conclusions until 1777, two or three years after most European scientists already knew about Priestley's work and had credited him with the discovery. It remained for another scientist to identify Priestley's dephlogisticated air as an element and to name it oxygen.

Antoine Lavoisier (1743–94), born to wealth and educated as a lawyer in France, began his scientific study at age twenty-one and came to doubt the phlogiston theory. The question was how to disprove it. In 1774, on a visit to France, Priestley met Lavoisier at a dinner party and told him about his discovery of dephlogisticated air. Coincidentally, shortly thereafter, Lavoisier received a letter from Scheele asking him to repeat one of his experiments that had produced "fire air." Lavoisier recognized the connection between the two men's experiments, tried them for himself, and named the resulting gas oxygen.

Who, then, is the real discoverer of oxygen—Karl Scheele, who first isolated it; Joseph Priestley, who first identified its properties; or Antoine Lavoisier, who named it? The best answer, perhaps, is all three. The important thing is that their work, taken together, launched the modern chemical revolution, which brought about massive transformations in industry, transportation, medicine, and every other aspect of life on the planet.

Antoine-Laurent Lavoisier. BLOCKER HISTORY OF MEDICINE COLLECTIONS, MOODY MEDICAL LIBRARY, THE UNIVERSITY OF TEXAS MEDICAL BRANCH, GALVESTON, TEXAS

PRIESTLEY, RATIONAL CHRISTIANITY, AND UNITARIANISM

Throughout his entire life, Joseph Priestley emphatically stated that his most important work was not his scientific research, but his work as a clergyman and theologian. At the same time, he also saw religion and science as complementary paths in his search for ultimate truth. Scientific experimentation, observation, and the power of reason, he believed, would validate the religious truths that had been revealed to the ancient Hebrews and the early Christians. Eventually, Priestley's quest for religious truth led him to believe in Unitarianism, which he called "rational Christianity," but which many of his contemporaries saw as one of the most dangerous, radical ideas of its time.

Priestley lived in a society that had already endured two centuries of debate, controversy, and even warfare over religion. After Henry VIII broke with the Catholic Church in 1534, and the ideas of the Protestant Reformation of Martin Luther and John Calvin began to spread throughout Europe, clergymen and lay believers in England had come to a variety of conclusions about what it meant to be a Christian. Some worked to reform the Church of England from within, while others became Separatists, trying to set an example from outside the established church. These nonconformists, or dissenters, eventually came to form new sects In Great Britain and its American colonies: Baptists, Congregationalists, Presbyterians, and Quakers in the seventeenth century; Shakers, Methodists, Universalists, and Unitarians in the eighteenth.

By the time Joseph Priestley was born, things had settled down quite a bit, but church and state were still closely linked in England and most of Anglo-America. Those in power firmly believed that a nation could not be stable without an established church in which all citizens shared the same faith. The Act of Toleration, passed in 1689, guaranteed all Protestants the right to practice their faith, though only members of the Church of England could participate fully in public life. Catholics and Jews had virtually no civil rights. Nonconformist Protestants could not hold public office. They had to pay taxes to support the Church of England, and then pay to support their own churches as well. Most dissenters disliked this second-class citizenship, but they accepted it. But the revolutions that created the United States and the French Republic dismantled established religion in those nations, which made Britain's dissenters hopeful and its establishment nervous.

Priestley and his brand of humanistic Unitarianism seemed especially dangerous because he labeled two long-held elements of church doctrine—the Trinity and the soul—as "the earliest and greatest corruptions" of Christianity. From his early years of questioning his family's Calvinist orthodoxy, Priestley sought to restore Christianity to its purest state, as revealed in the Bible and understood by human reason, without the superstitions that mere human beings had imposed on it. He traced the concept of a soul, separate from the human

conception of air as a combination of gases, with oxygen as the vital element in the burning process. Up until that time, the prevailing theory was that flammable objects contained a substance called "phlogiston," which was released into the air during combustion. Lavoisier proposed instead that burning objects did not release a gas, but rather absorbed the oxygen in the air—a theory that was soon accepted as scientific fact. Priestley, though, had an obstinate streak, and in spite of all evidence to the contrary, he stuck to his notion of oxygen as "dephlogisticated air" for the rest of his life, while the rest of the scientific world turned to Lavoisier's new theories. Nonetheless, it was Priestley's singular achievement to be the first to isolate oxygen and to identify its essential properties.

body, to the ancient Greeks, not the Bible. Nor could he find any biblical evidence for the idea of the Trinity, an essential element of the doctrine of most Protestant sects, as well as the Catholic Church. According to Unitarians, the concept that three entities—Father, Son, and Holy Spirit—could be incorporated into one God contradicted reason and relied on blind faith, which made it anathema to rational Christians.

Priestley did not make this leap from the Calvinist orthodoxy of his birth family in one fell swoop. For a time, in the early years of his ministry, he adhered to Arianism, which was more moderate than Unitarianism but still a rank heresy in the eyes of many other Christians. Arians believed that the Son and Holy Spirit were subordinate to God the Father, though they had existed before the creation of the universe. Unitarians, in the most humanistic form that Priestley adopted, held that only God the Father is divine, that the Holy Spirit represents the will of God expressed on earth, and that Jesus was fully human, albeit a human with a special mission, divinely selected to demonstrate how people should live and to assure them of resurrection.

Unlike many later Unitarians, Priestley continued to believe in the coming millennium, when God's kingdom would be restored on earth and all believers would be resurrected. The American and French Revolutions were, to him, potential signs that those times were at hand. As the earliest region of America to dispense fully with an established church, and the one offering the broadest religious freedom, Pennsylvania seemed the place where Joseph Priestley would feel most at home.

The Mystical Divine. Priestley was lampooned for his subversive beliefs in dozens of English cartoons, such as this one in which he explains away the Bible and burns the documents of established political and religious thought. CHEMICAL HERITAGE FOUNDATION IMAGE ARCHIVES, OTHMER LIBRARY OF CHEMICAL HISTORY, PHILADELPHIA

FREETHINKING AND ITS CONSEQUENCES

Shelburne remarried in 1779, and Priestley fell into disfavor at Bowood soon afterward, perhaps because the new Lady Shelburne objected to his radical religious ideas. The following year, Priestley left the earl's service and moved to the outskirts of Birmingham, where he and his family established a home. He and Mary now had four children; Henry, the youngest and the last, had been born in 1777. Unlike Joseph's mother, who died young from "having children so fast" (six within seven years), Mary Priestley's childbirths had been carefully spaced out, with three to six years between each.

Priestley received a lifetime pension from Shelburne, and various friends and relatives contributed to support his sci-

The Birmingham Riots. In England, known sympathizers of the French Revolution, such as Priestley, became targets of violent mobs. His house at Fair Hill was looted and burned during an uprising at Birmingham in 1791. ARCHIVES AND SPECIAL COLLECTIONS, DICKINSON COLLEGE, CARLISLE, PENNSYLVANIA

entific work so that he did not need to search for a position as a teacher or minister. Mary's brother, John Wilkinson, who had become a wealthy steel manufacturer, provided a house, and Josiah Wedgwood, founder of the famous pottery manufacturing company, contributed money and laboratory equipment. Other men and women provided for him as well: A Mrs. Rayner was his "chief benefactress," and Mr. Parker, a London glassmaker, donated whatever glass equipment Priestley needed.

In Birmingham, Priestley joined a circle of men called the Lunar Society, also known as the "Lunatics," who met to discuss literature, science, and issues of the day. The group included not only Wedgwood, but also James Watt and Matthew Boulton, who were developing the steam engine, and Erasmus Darwin, grandfather of Charles Darwin (who developed the theory of evolution). This was, he later recalled, the happiest time

of his life. In this congenial atmosphere, Priestley continued his prolific writing and published several controversial pamphlets and books on theology. In *History of the Corruptions of Christianity* and *History of the Early Opinions Concerning Jesus Christ,* he laid out his belief that the concept of God as a Trinity was mistaken and not according to Scripture. This was a direct attack on the established church, and clergymen and politicians alike denounced the author of the pamphlets. The popular *Gentleman's Magazine* alone carried dozens of articles railing against him. In 1785, Priestley published a sermon on *The Importance and Extent of Free Enquiry in Matters of Religion,* in which he declared that he and other dissenters were "laying gunpowder, grain by grain, under the old building of error and superstition." He was speaking metaphorically, but the phrase earned him the nickname "Gunpowder Joe" and made him seem potentially dangerous.

Like other English radicals and many Americans, Priestley welcomed the French Revolution of 1789. But those in power feared the spread of revolution and a possible invasion by France, and British authorities suspected anyone who praised the French Revolution of plotting treason. On July 14, 1791, a group of eighty men met for dinner to celebrate Bastille Day, the anniversary of the French Revolution. Priestley's sympathies lay with the group, although he did not attend the dinner himself. A group of protestors gathered to demonstrate their disapproval of the radicals. After the dinner group broke up, the protesters turned nasty and marched on the New Meetinghouse, where Priestley had often preached, and burned it to the ground. They then ransacked the Priestleys' house and set it on fire, destroying the laboratory and library, including

some manuscripts that had not yet been published. Priestley and his family escaped in the nick of time with only the clothes they were wearing.

Priestley fled to London and never returned to Birmingham. He received letters of support from America, and the French Assembly voted to make him an honorary citizen of France. In London, a small group of friends helped his family get settled, but he faced a great deal of hostility, with denunciations in the House of Commons and pulpits throughout Britain. Newspapers caricatured him, and crowds burned him in effigy. Priestley was convinced, probably justifiably, that church and political leaders had fomented the riots against him. At the very least, the government failed to protect him against mob violence, and the courts awarded him damages of several thousand pounds in compensation for his losses—although much of what he had lost was irreplaceable, not least of all his family's peace of mind. In a classic case of blaming the victim for violence committed against him, even his colleagues at the Royal Society snubbed him, and he was forced to resign.

PRIESTLEY IN AMERICA

The question now was no longer whether to emigrate, but where the family could go. They thought first of France. One son, William, was already there and had become a naturalized French citizen. The French Assembly made Priestley an honorary citizen, and he had investments there. But the French Revolution was becoming brutal; even Lavoisier was about to meet his death at the guillotine. Priestley and his family thought increasingly of America. In 1793, Joseph Jr. and Henry, along with family friend Thomas Cooper, left for the United States, where William soon joined them. For a year, the young men explored various regions in

the new nation, with the goal of establishing a settlement for refugee English dissenters. They finally decided on central Pennsylvania, where they found what was perhaps the largest single unsold parcel of land in the Northeast, located between the North and West Branches of the Susquehanna River. At the time, the town nearest to the projected settlement was Northumberland, and Joseph Jr. and his wife, Elizabeth Ryland Priestley, established a home there, as did his younger brothers.

By 1794, Joseph and Mary Priestley had decided to immigrate to Pennsylvania to be near their children and to escape the bigotry of England. They arrived in New York on June 4, and then traveled to Philadelphia, with a brief stop in between to visit the college at Princeton, New Jersey. On June 25, the *Pennsylvania Gazette* announced, "Last Thursday evening arrived in town from

Thomas Cooper. *The radical comrade of Priestley immigrated to America and settled in Northumberland for a time. He was a political activist, lawyer, physician, scientist, and teacher. This portrait was painted by Charles Willson Peale (1741–1827) in 1819.* MÜTTER MUSEUM, COLLEGE OF PHYSICIANS OF PHILADELPHIA

PRIESTLEY, PANTISOCRACY, AND
THE LOYALSOCK LANDS

The Birmingham riots and fire transformed Priestley into a martyr and a hero to a new generation of British radicals. Two young poets, Samuel Taylor Coleridge (1772–1834) and Robert Southey (1774–1843), were particularly enraged by the bigotry and superstition that "have driven our PRIESTLEY o'er the Ocean swell," as Coleridge put it in his December 1794 poem "Priestley." Coleridge and Southey hoped to join Priestley in rural Pennsylvania, where they planned to establish a utopian community called Pantisocracy, from the Greek meaning "equal rule of all."

In early 1794, Priestley's young friend Thomas Cooper returned to England with glowing reports of the large, unsettled tract of land north of Northumberland, along Loyalsock Creek and the North Branch of the Susquehanna, beginning about fifty miles due north of Northumberland. Cooper published a pamphlet, *Some Information Respecting America*, advertising the land and offering it for sale to prospective settlers and investors. The publication took the form of a letter to "A Friend," understood by all to be Joseph Priestley. Cooper believed that if the great man emigrated, many like-minded English families would follow. The inhabitants of the seven hundred thousand acres eventually patented by the Priestleys and their friends were to be English-born gentlemen farmers. The lands were to be purchased at thirty shillings an acre, and the main profits would come from selling surplus lands once communities began to develop and prosper. Most of the lands were never paid for, and eventually the whole scheme fell apart. But for about a year, hopes were high.

Coleridge and Southey seized on Cooper's pamphlet and immediately began recruiting friends for their own community, probably to be located on North Branch lands near Asylum, where French Royalists fleeing the guillotine had been offered a refuge (where they hoped Marie Antoinette would join them). By the end of 1794, the poets had twelve couples lined up—everyone was to be married—and had come up with a schedule and plan for their new society. Each family would have four hundred acres to farm, but there would be ample workers for hire, so the poets and their friends would have to work for only two or three hours a day themselves. The rest of the time would be spent in cultivation of the mind, and there would be a fine library for that purpose. Women, of course, would care for the children, but they, too, would spend the rest of their time in thought and study. This was clearly not the most practical plan in the world, but the poets waxed enthusiastic. "This new pantisocratic scheme," Southey wrote, "had given me new life, new hope, new energy; all the faculties of my mind are dilated." Coleridge gushed in print, "Yet will I love to follow the sweet dream, / Where Susquehannak pours his untam'd stream."

Money was the only sticking point in these romantic visions. Cooper's pamphlet emphasized the need for each immigrant to arrive with sufficient money and goods to get started, but Southey and Coleridge were both poor. In early New York, the justly celebrated Philosopher, Doctor Joseph Priestley." In Philadelphia, America's leading intelligentsia welcomed the distinguished immigrant. London's Royal Society may have rejected him, but Philadelphia's American Philosophical Society rejoiced at having him in their midst. He had been elected a member of America's premier scientific association in 1786, while Franklin was still alive (he had died in 1790). Now Dr. Benjamin Rush and his colleagues urged him to settle in the city. Rush had achieved fame as the heroic medical man who had stayed in the city during the yellow fever epidemic of the previous summer, when other doctors fled to escape the contagion.

Priestley thought seriously about setting up house on the outskirts of the

Samuel Taylor Coleridge and Robert Southey. The poets, then in their early twenties, were painted by Peter Vandyke (1729–99) in 1795, the same year they had planned to join their hero Priestley in Pennsylvania. NATIONAL PORTRAIT GALLERY, LONDON

1795, they embarked on a lecture series in Bristol, England, on history, politics, and morality. The series ended badly when Coleridge failed to show up for his final performance, probably because he was lost in a haze from smoking the opium pipe he had begun using as a college student.

When their intended departure time of March 1795 arrived, the poets did not have nearly enough money. They continued to cling to their dream of a utopia amid the Susquehanna's "excessive beauty," but the closest they actually came to communal life was when they married two sisters, Edith and Sarah Fricker, and the couples lived together in England for a short while.

Perhaps it was all for the best. The poets were like the majority of Englishmen who came to America, Priestley said, "with such erroneous ideas" that they were "ill qualified to commence cultivation in a wilderness." The result would have been even more criticism and abuse for Priestley and company for what were simply "their well-meant endeavours to promote the interests of their countrymen."

Source: Mary Cathryne Park, "Joseph Priestley and the Problem of Pantisocracy." *Proceedings of the Delaware County Institute of Science* 11, no. 1 (1947).

city, perhaps in Germantown, but his wife had other ideas. She developed "an unconquerable aversion to Philadelphia" and preferred to live in the countryside. The family made the difficult five-day trip to Northumberland, overland in two wagons most of the way, except where the creeks were swollen and canoes ferried them over with their baggage. When they first arrived in Northumberland, the doctor was a bit disappointed at the primitive state of the town and was still thinking about the amenities of city life. In the end, he concluded that since what he called his "evil genius" had brought them across the ocean, he had to leave the choice of their place of residence to his wife. For her part, Mary thought the area was "very delightful," with "more beautiful"

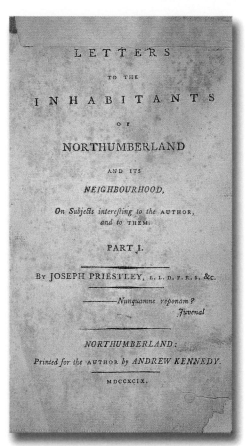

Letters to the Inhabitants of Northumberland and Its Neighbourhood. *Priestley declared his allegiances and explained his intentions in America in this 1801 pamphlet.* JOSEPH PRIESTLEY HOUSE

woods and rivers than she had ever seen. Her husband settled down and contented himself with the thought of annual trips to Philadelphia.

In spring 1795, Joseph Priestley and his daughter-in-law returned to Philadelphia, where he was invited to preach at Philadelphia's Universalist Church. The doctor made three more visits to the city, in 1796, 1801, and 1803. There, he was able to meet with fellow scientists and philosophers to discuss the latest discoveries, attend various churches and give an occasional sermon, debate theology and politics, and renew friendships. A stagecoach began operating between Philadelphia and Northumberland in 1797, but the trip still took five days, and there was still no bridge or frequent ferry service across the Susquehanna to Northumberland. So for the most part, Priestley contented himself with remaining at home, where he busied himself with reading, writing, and scientific experimentation. His most notable scientific discovery during these years was the discovery and isolation of a new gas, carbon monoxide, in 1799.

Early on in the ten years he spent in the United States, Priestley was hopeful, writing his friends in England that his new home promised "to be a happy asylum during the troubles in Europe." Unfortunately, some of Europe's troubles soon followed him to America, when another English immigrant, William Cobbett, using the pen name of Peter Porcupine, wrote a pamphlet accusing the doctor of being a traitor and a French spy who should not be allowed to become a naturalized American citizen. Priestley defended himself by pointing out that although he celebrated both the French and American Revolutions, he was a loyal Englishman and had no intention of becoming a naturalized citizen of the United States. In his own pamphlet, *Letters to the Inhabitants of Northumberland and Its Neighborhood* (1801), Priestley said that he was merely "an inhabitant" and "a peaceable stranger" interested in the welfare of the new nation and would do whatever he could "to promote its prosperity." His main contribution, he said, would "chiefly consist in giving my honest opinion."

Unfortunately, during the administration of John Adams (1797–1801),

honest opinions were not always welcome. The Alien and Sedition Acts subjected noncitizens to deportation if they voiced any criticism of the government, a clear violation of the First Amendment's guarantee of freedom of speech. At some risk of being deported, Priestley continued to defend free speech and free thought. After Thomas Jefferson took office in 1801 and the acts were repealed, Priestley wrote with some satisfaction that for the first time in his life, he was living under a government he respected, because it respected the freedom of all its inhabitants.

He was not so fortunate in his personal life, where the sorrows seem to have outweighed the joys. Just a year and a half after his arrival in America, his youngest son, Henry, died. His beloved "Harry" had shown some aptitude for scholarly work, and the doctor had high hopes for him. Less than two months later, Harry's older brother William married a native-born woman, Margaret Foulke, in Harrisburg; this marriage, during what should have been a period of mourning, may have been a source of disagreement between father and son. The following year, 1796, the family faced more sorrow when Mary Priestley died. After doing so much of the planning for the new house, she did not live to move into it. Instead, in 1798, Joseph Jr., his wife, and two young children moved with Priestley to the new house.

Another blow came in 1800, when William had a complete falling out with his father and moved away from Northumberland, first to his wife's birthplace, and then to Louisiana, where he eventually became a wealthy planter. The rupture created rumors, which were published in a Reading newspaper, that William had tried to poison his father and the rest of the household. William denied the charges, and his father came to his defense and said that he felt "more compassion than resentment" for his son. Still, the doctor admitted, "I do not expect or wish to see him any more." The losses were offset in some measure by the presence of grandchildren. Three of Elizabeth Ryland Priestley's children—Joseph Rayner, Elizabeth, and Lindsey—seem to have been a great comfort to their grandfather in his later years.

In 1801, during a trip to Philadelphia, Joseph Priestley became seriously ill with a respiratory illness, perhaps pneumonia, and he never fully regained his health. The following year, he was forced to admit that he had begun to lose his hearing and ordered an ear trumpet. Soon afterward, he fell and injured his hip, but he was still able to get around on crutches. In 1803, he made one last visit to Philadelphia, where he spoke to the Unitarian Society and was the guest of honor at a dinner given by the American Philosophical Society. On his return to Northumberland, he was so weakened that he took to sleeping on a bed in his library to avoid having to climb the stairs. He continued to work on his writing up until the end, which came on February 6, 1804. He died in his library at age seventy, shortly after dictating some changes in a manuscript to his son Joseph Jr.

History of the Joseph Priestley House

B y the time Joseph Priestley came to live in Northumberland in 1794, the central Susquehanna Valley had seen human activity for some twelve thousand years. The continent's native peoples had been hunting, fishing, and gathering wild foods in the region for at least that long. Native women and men had been farming the lands—growing corn, squash, and beans—for more than three thousand years. The point where the North and West Branches join together to form a single Susquehanna River (at the present-day towns of Sunbury, Northumberland, and Shamokin Dam) was an especially advantageous spot marking the juncture of several important Indian east-west and north-south travel and trade routes. During the first half of the eighteenth century, this was the site of Shamokin (now Sunbury), the largest and most important Indian trading town, where the Oneida leader Shikellamy presided over a mixed community of Iroquois, Delawares, Tutelos, and others. By 1725, French Huguenot trader James Le Tort had a trading house on the site where Northumberland would be established. In the 1740s, the leg-

endary Madame Montour and Andrew Montour, métis (French-Indian) interpreters for the Pennsylvania government, lived on the Big Island between Sunbury and Northumberland.

During the Seven Years' War, the region's native population fled west and north; after the war ended in 1763, German, Scots-Irish, and other European immigrants came into the area in increasing numbers. A small number of African Americans, most of them slaves, also came to live and work. Northumberland was initially formed in 1772, and in 1774 a Quaker brewer from Germantown, outside Philadelphia, received a patent to lay out the town and sell lots. He chose a traditional English pattern of houses surrounding a village green, and within twenty years the infant settlement had some one hundred houses. When it was completed in 1798, Joseph Priestley's house would be the largest and finest of them all.

When they first arrived in Northumberland in 1794, Joseph and Mary Priestley lived with their son Joseph Jr. while they decided where to establish their residence. At first the whole family had intended to settle farther north, on

Priestley's Library.

a large, unoccupied tract of land in which they had invested with their friend Thomas Cooper, who had immigrated in 1793 with the Priestleys' sons. But more investors and settlers were needed, and it soon became clear that there would not be enough of either. Mary Priestley vehemently rejected the idea of returning to Philadelphia—it was too unhealthy, too expensive, and too crowded—and her husband acceded to her wish to remain in Northumberland, where there were at least some amenities of community life, such as a general store, and the promise of more to come: A post office would open; stagecoaches and wagons would start to travel back and forth to Philadelphia with passengers, freight, mail, and newspapers; a new school, Northumberland Academy, was in the works; and Northumberland might even become the new state capital. Much of this never materialized, at least not as soon as the Priestleys hoped, but they continued to have high hopes for the place they now called home.

DESIGN OF THE HOUSE

While her husband studied, wrote books and sermons, and rambled in the woods in search of botanical samples, Mary Priestley set about planning and designing their new home. "She has taken much pleasure in planning the new house," he wrote, "and it promises to be everything she asked it to be." She probably worked with local carpenter-builders and an English architectural pattern book; many such books had been published in England since the early eighteenth century. At the time, America had few trained architects, and apprenticeship with an established architect was the only way to receive training. Not until the 1850s did the United States have formal institutions for teaching young, would-be architects. In fact, the noted American architect H. H. Richardson (1838–86), Mary and Joseph Priestley's great-grandson, opened one of the first such architectural training schools.

The earliest known architectural rendering of the Priestley house dates from 1800, after the house was completed. In 1983, Pennsylvania Historical and Museum Commission (PHMC) researchers visiting the Royal Society of Chemistry in London discovered a watercolor of the house and its landscape, signed by a person known only as T. Lambourne, a surveyor from Luzerne County. Whether Lambourne had a role in designing or building the house, or simply painted it for the family after the fact, is unknown.

Mary Priestley. Though she died before the house was completed, Priestley's wife was largely responsible for its design.
HARRIS MANCHESTER COLLEGE, OXFORD

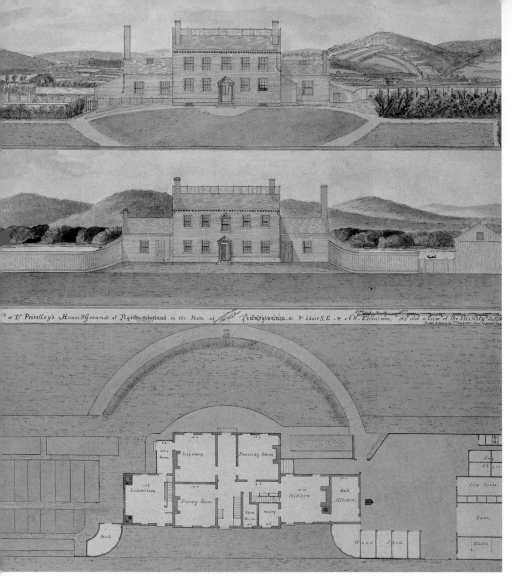

Plan and Elevation for Joseph Priestley House, c. 1800. *This watercolor, signed T. Lambourne, was discovered at the Royal Society of Chemistry in London by PHMC researchers. It has served as a key resource in today's interpretation of the Priestley House.*

PENNSYLVANIA HISTORICAL AND MUSEUM COMMISSION

Joseph Priestley himself probably had more to do with the design of the house, especially his library and laboratory, than his extant letters reveal. Much to his delight, by 1797, the laboratory became the first wing of the house to be completed—a good indication of what his priorities were. He took great pride in his library and "philosophical apparatus," or scientific equipment, which he believed were "superior to anything of the kind in this country." For the first time in his life, he had a laboratory that he had designed, built, and outfitted entirely himself. This was deeply gratifying, especially after losing everything in the Birmingham riots just six years earlier.

WHY DID THE PRIESTLEYS CHOOSE NORTHUMBERLAND?

Why did Joseph Priestley, called "one of the greatest men alive" by his peers, decide to settle in the tiny rural town of Northumberland? This is the first question asked by many of today's visitors to his house; it was also something many of his contemporaries questioned. In fact, he may occasionally have asked himself the same thing, especially when he realized that mail could take months to come from England, sometimes weeks just to arrive from Philadelphia. One package of books he had ordered was delivered to Carlisle by mistake, and it took nearly two years to get to him. But for Joseph Priestley, and even more for his wife, Mary, the Susquehanna Valley had virtues that, in the end, outweighed its failings.

Over the centuries, immigrants came to America for a variety of reasons, often oversimplified as either purely religious or purely economic. In reality, people usually came because of mixed motives. "Push" factors, like religious persecution, political repression, and economic hardship, propelled men and women to leave the old country, while "pull" factors, such as religious and political freedom and economic opportunity, led them to the new land. Immigrants usually chose specific destinations because they had friends or family members already there who wrote them glowing reports, emphasizing the positive and minimizing the negative aspects of America.

The Birmingham riots and fire were clearly the immediate push factor driving the Priestleys to leave England. But the mob violence stood for larger forces of popular bigotry, lack of freedom of speech, and continuing discrimination against religious dissenters. Priestley had long extolled the cause of America and the religious and political freedoms that it represented. But he and his sons also saw financial opportunity in Pennsylvania, in the tract of land they hoped to develop into a refuge for English dissidents like themselves. Priestley's goal was not to become wealthy, as many of America's land speculators were doing, but simply to live a comfortable life and be able to pursue his experimentation and writing without having to worry about the size of his income.

Mary and Joseph Priestley went to Northumberland at first simply because their sons were there and had written to them about the advantages of the region. They stayed on because it met their most basic requirements more than any alternative location. It was everything that Philadelphia was not. In Joseph Priestley's view, the city was "unpleasant, unhealthy, and intolerably expensive; and there I should have little command of my time." Land was cheap in the central Susquehanna Valley. Here the Priestleys and their sons could afford to buy property for their own houses and to hold as investments. Soon after their arrival, they paid thirty shillings an acre for three hundred acres of land, an almost unbelievable bargain compared with property in England or any of America's more settled areas.

Northumberland was also a healthy environment, both physically and spiritually, in which Joseph and Mary could enjoy their later years and their sons could mature and raise

The exterior and plan of the house are typically Georgian in style, with some decorative elements more characteristic of the Federal style of architecture. The Georgian style had developed in England during the eighteenth century and was imported into the American colonies. Georgian houses were characterized by a subdued elegance, with balance and symmetry in both plan and exterior appearance. In the late eighteenth century, English architect Robert Adam began to use elements inspired by the ancient Greeks and Romans, and Americans adapted the Adam style into a Federal style suitable, they believed, for a new

Northumberland, 1798. Le Comte Colbert de Maulevrier documented Priestley's neighborhood along the Susquehanna in the year that the house, to the right, was completed. PENNSYLVANIA HISTORICAL AND MUSEUM COMMISSION

their own families. The year before the Priestleys arrived, Philadelphia had suffered the worst yellow fever epidemic in its history. Wealthy families fled the city for their country estates, but most working people had no alternative but to stay in the city and see the disease infect their families and neighbors by the hundreds. The Priestleys did not care for the social environment of the city, either. They had expected to see traditional Quaker simplicity, but instead they found hypocrisy. Wealthy Quakers kept up the formality of their tradition and dressed in austere colors, but they lived opulent lives, in ostentatious houses with elaborate furnishings, and seemed to care only about making more money.

Finally, Joseph Priestley had far more control over his own time in Northumberland than he would have had in Philadelphia. Although he enjoyed the company of his fellow philosophers in the city, he was content to limit that pleasure to occasional visits. In his new home along the Susquehanna, the doctor had the peace and quiet he needed to write and perform his experiments. On her part, Mary Priestley had the pleasure of being near her sons and one grandchild (she had left her daughter, Sarah, and other grandchildren behind in England).

republic. The Priestley House includes delicate Federal-style details, such as the fanlights over the doors and the balustrades on the rooftop belvedere and main staircase, but it does not use the more elaborate elements of the style—for example, a massive portico supported by columns—typical of the houses Priestley's contemporaries were building. In keeping with Priestley's desire for simplicity, it continues the Georgian dedication to balance, with symmetrical windows, doors, and flanking wings, with only the barest ornamentation.

Brick, or brick and stone, were the usual building materials for fine Geor-

gian and Federal buildings, but in rural Northumberland, the only plentiful, and therefore affordable, material was wood, harvested from Pennsylvania's lush forests. Even seasoned lumber was not easy to procure, and the wood had to be kiln-dried for ten days, ten thousand feet at a time, in two-foot-deep trenches. Priestley concluded, perhaps somewhat defensively, "A house constructed with such boards I prefer to one of brick and stone."

The Lambourne plan indicates the location of outbuildings and fences that had been long gone by the 1960s. The renderings of the front and back of the house show its setting in the eighteenth-century landscape, with sweeping vistas of river and mountains. These panoramic views were a major factor in drawing the Priestleys to settle on this site. Nowhere in England or in the more settled parts of America could this family of moderate means have afforded to live amid such desirable scenery.

When it was finished in 1798, Joseph Priestley was justifiably proud of his new home, though he admitted that it was perhaps a bit "too aristocratical for the habitation of a democrat." He became quite annoyed when critic William Cobbett called his home a mere "shed which I dignify with the name of a house." Cobbett clearly had not seen the house for himself, although he probably had heard that it was built of wood, not the brick or stone that an English builder would have used. But in nearly all other respects, the exterior of Priestley's new home resembled the Georgian manor house of an English country gentleman of moderate means.

SUBSEQUENT HISTORY

Like many historic houses, the Joseph Priestley House has had a checkered history since its most famous occupant died there two hundred years ago. It has seen many owners and occupants, been subjected to a variety of renovations, and served multiple functions. Since 1968, the PHMC has been working to restore the house and landscape as closely as possible to its appearance from 1798 to 1804, when Joseph Priestley lived and worked there. But evidence of the house's subsequent history will remain after even the most complete restoration, so it is important that visitors be aware of the site's entire history.

After Priestley's death, family members continued to live in the house until 1811, when Joseph Priestley Jr. and his wife, Elizabeth Ryland, decided to move back to England and sell the house. Before the end of the nineteenth century, the house was sold a total of six times. Judge Seth Chapman purchased the house in 1815 and lived in it until his death in 1835. James Kay, the Unitarian minister in Northumberland, lived in the house after that, and his son Charles bought the property in 1847. Henry Campbell bought the house in 1865, only to sell it three years later to Hugh Johnston. In 1888, Johnston sold it to Kate Scott. When the Pennsylvania Railroad began building its yards in Northumberland in 1910, Scott turned the building into a boardinghouse for railroad workers.

Although the house remained in private hands all this time, it held special significance for one group of Americans—the founders of the American Chemical Society, now the world's largest professional membership organization devoted to a single science. In 1874, seventy-seven chemists made a pilgrimage to the site to celebrate the centennial of chemistry. When the group met in Philadelphia in 1926, the scien-

tists chartered a train to Northumberland to commemorate their initial meeting more than half a century earlier and dedicate a small museum built on the grounds of the Priestley House.

CREATING A MUSEUM

A chemistry professor was the first person to express interest in establishing a museum at the Priestley House. The house came up for sale at auction in 1919, and the successful bidder was Dr. George Gilbert Pond, professor of chemistry and dean of the School of Natural Sciences at Pennsylvania State College (now Penn State University). Pond had raised the funds from his colleagues and former students, with the intention of moving the house to the State College campus, about eighty miles away, where it could serve as offices of the Chemistry Department. The college trustees agreed to care for the house once it was moved, but they never provided funds for moving it to its new site, so it stayed put.

When Pond died just a year after buying the property, a memorial association and fund were established to restore the house where it stood and to build a fireproof museum for Priestley's books and scientific equipment. Throughout the years that the college owned the house, it served as a museum, with resident caretakers for much of that time. In 1955, the college gave the property over to the borough of Northumberland, which used it for offices for four years, until it became clear that maintenance costs were too high. In 1959, the Pennsylvania General Assembly mandated the acquisition and maintenance of the property by the PHMC. In 1965, the house was designated as a National Historic Landmark, and in 1968 the PHMC began to restore the property systematically, replacing windows, returning door-

The Second-Floor Bedroom exhibits furnishings and possessions that would likely be found in the chamber of an eighteenth-century woman of the stature of Elizabeth Ryland Priestley, the doctor's daughter-in-law and mistress of the house.

ways to their original locations, and removing Victorian-era ornamentation that had been added over the years. Two years later, the property was rededicated as the Joseph Priestley House and opened to the public.

Until the discovery of the Lambourne watercolor, the PHMC staff had almost no documentation for the layout of the property or the function that each room served in Priestley's time. The dis-

Furnace Foundations *were uncovered during an excavation of the Priestley laboratory in 1995.*

covery of the original plan in 1983 led to some reinterpretation and additional restoration. Adjacent to the existing structure, PHMC archaeologists uncovered the foundations of the carriage barn and privies shown in the plan, and these were rebuilt according to their original dimensions. The reconstructed barn now serves as a visitor center.

As is the case with most historic houses, the original occupants' furniture did not remain in the house after it was sold. The PHMC faced a daunting task in reassembling furniture and artifacts for the house, especially since no inventory of the Priestley family's possessions there was ever taken. The only extant inventory of Joseph Priestley's furniture, books, and other belongings was the one he made to record his losses in the Birmingham fire of 1791. That inventory gives researchers a guide to the sort of furniture that he probably had in Northumberland as

well: simple, but in good taste for the period. Penn State University, during its ownership of the house, had acquired some items for exhibition, mostly books and personal items, such as Priestley's hickory cane and a signet fob given him by the Royal Society. Descendants of Joseph and Mary Priestley, from their current homes scattered across the globe, have donated heirlooms that have been in the family at least since Joseph Priestley Jr.'s lifetime.

In the 1990s, the PHMC initiated two projects as part of the Pennsylvania Humanities Council's "Raising Our Sites" program. The goal was to illuminate the lives of those less well-known historic groups, in this case, the women and servants who lived and worked in the house. Several years of research resulted in a total makeover of the second-floor bedroom, to reflect the daily activities of an eighteenth-century

woman and the children and servants who were primarily in her care. Since Mary Priestley had died before the family moved into the house, the room reflects the life of her daughter-in-law, Elizabeth Ryland Priestley, who served as the mistress of the house during the time that Dr. Priestley lived there.

A second grant began with a tantalizingly brief 1795 notation by Joseph Priestley, stating that in the absence of a full-time, live-in maidservant, "we only hire a black slave by the week." Slavery is not included in the usual histories of central Pennsylvania, but it was part of the economic and social structure of the region during Priestley's lifetime. Finding white women and men willing to work as servants was difficult enough in Philadelphia; they were even scarcer in rural areas. While still in England, Priestley had spoken out against the slave trade, and he apparently never owned slaves himself, but the realities of America's labor scarcity did apparently lead his family to "rent" one enslaved person. Priestley's friend Thomas Cooper, who had also written against slavery, became a full-fledged slaveowner once he moved to South Carolina. Like Thomas Jefferson and many other intellectuals of the

day, Joseph Priestley and his cohort display a certain disjunction between theory and practice. Opposed to slavery in principle, the Priestley family still made use of slave labor.

The PHMC's restoration work has continued with archaeological and architectural investigation of Dr. Priestley's laboratory, which uncovered the foundations of the furnaces at either end of the room and suggest a panel construction of the exterior wall, possibly designed to bear the brunt of any explosion that might result from chemical experiments.

The American Chemical Society has continued its close relationship with the site. On two occasions in 1974, the bicentennial of the discovery of oxygen, several hundred chemists made pilgrimages to the house. Two years later, the society celebrated its own centennial with a special meeting in Northumberland and arranged for Corning Glass to reproduce Priestley's eighteenth-century laboratory glassware for display at the site. In 1994, as part of an international educational program, the society designated the Joseph Priestley House as a National Historic Chemical Landmark.

Visiting the Site

SITE LEGEND

1 Visitor Center

2 Courtyard

3 Facade and Landscape

4 Entry Hall

5 Library

6 Laboratory

7 Drawing Room

8 Main Kitchen

9 Back Kitchen

10 Dining Room

11 Stairway and Upstairs Hall

12 Bedchamber

13 Pond Building

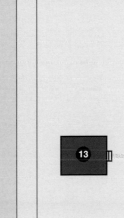

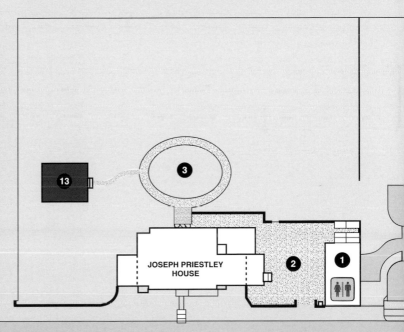

HANOVER ST.

13

3

JOSEPH PRIESTLEY
HOUSE

2

1

PRIESTLEY AVE.

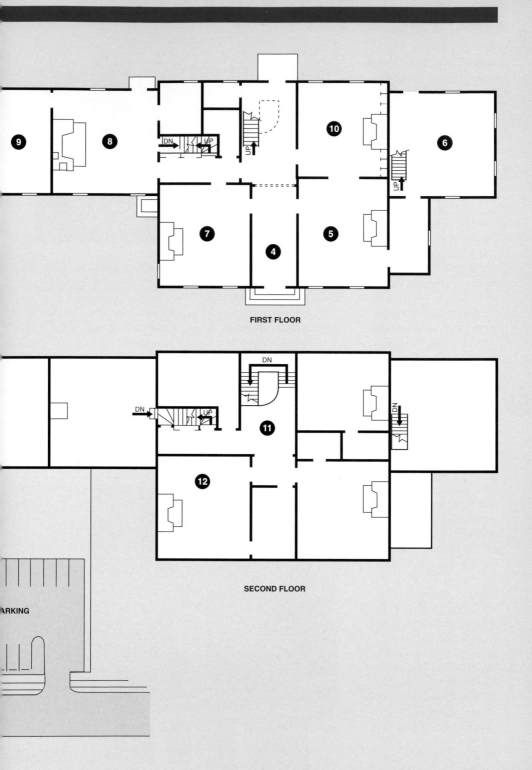

FIRST FLOOR

SECOND FLOOR

PARKING

35

① VISITOR CENTER

Tours of the Joseph Priestley House begin at the Visitor Center, a 1999 replica of Joseph Priestley's 1798 carriage house. Here visitors can obtain tickets for guided tours and find public restrooms. The small bookstore sells biographies of Priestley, as well as books and pamphlets about the history of the region and eighteenth-century English Enlightenment, of which Priestley was so much a part.

When the PHMC acquired the site in 1959, the barn was no longer standing, but archaeological and manuscript research revealed its existence. The current structure stands on the architectural "footprint" of the original building, and its appearance is an approximation of what the original building must have looked like. The only known depiction of the barn is the Lambourne rendering of 1800, which shows it as a wooden construction divided into a stable, a barn, and a "cow house."

② COURTYARD

The courtyard contains replicas of several outbuildings that, like the barn, did not survive into the mid-twentieth century. A woodshed attached to the back kitchen provided protection from the elements for firewood, the sole source of fuel for cooking, baking, and heating the house, which had a fireplace in nearly every room. The wood also fueled two furnaces in the laboratory. Pigsties stand adjacent to the river side of the property, and next to them are two freestanding double privies (outhouses). An archaeological dig in 1986 confirmed the presence of the outdoor bake oven depicted in the Lambourne drawing. An outdoor oven would have kept the house cooler in the summer and lessened the danger of fire, an ever-present hazard for wood houses. Archaeologists also excavated a cistern in the courtyard that existed before the mid-nineteenth century, possibly during the Priestleys' residence.

FACADE AND LANDSCAPE

Joseph Priestley designed his house to face the river, in the traditional Anglo-American fashion of his time. There was a practical reason for the front

door to be on the river side of the house: Many travelers arrived by boat or ferry rather than by overland transport. But by the late eighteenth century, there was also an aesthetic reason: The prevailing wisdom was that the view from a country house should be an open landscape vista rather than a townscape. In fact, Priestley walled off the town with a high, wooden privacy wall that can be seen in the Lambourne drawing. Atop the roof, he installed a narrow railed walkway as a belvedere, from the Latin for "beautiful view," to command a panoramic view of the surrounding countryside.

The view of the Susquehanna River has changed markedly since Priestley's lifetime. Originally the property encompassed two and a half

acres and took in all the lands down to the riverbank. Instead of Priestley's unobstructed view, the modern visitor sees railroad tracks, chain-link fencing, playing fields, and a concession stand. Priestley's conception of landscape design for his property was perhaps a much scaled-down version of the beautiful gardens he had known during his years working at Lord Shelburne's estate of Bowood, in Wiltshire, England. There the virtuoso English landscape architect Capability Brown had created one of his finest designs, with gently sloping lawns from the house to the lake, much as Priestley's Northumberland lawn sloped down to the river. The doctor clearly enjoyed his new surroundings, from carefully pruned fruit-bearing trees

near the house to the wilder neighboring woods. He wrote to invite English friends to visit and join him on "walks along the banks of the Susquehanna and ramble . . . in the woods."

Priestley's new house was a pragmatic but aesthetic mix of the prevailing Georgian and Federal styles of architecture. The plan, balanced and symmetrical in most respects, was typically Georgian, while many of the decorative elements, such as the fanlight and arch over the front door, were taken from the Federal vocabulary. Brick or stone were the preferred building materials, but Priestley soon found them unavailable or unaffordable in Northumberland, so he used the plentiful timber of the region to clothe the house in clapboard. Two tiers of twelve-pane windows flank the front door in perfect symmetry, four on each side and one above the front door. On either side of the two-story building are one-story wings, one housing the kitchens and the other Priestley's laboratory. The wings are perfectly matched structures except for the addition of a passageway for the doctor to pass easily from his library to his laboratory. The chimneys, too, are balanced on the facade of the main central portion of the house, one on either side. Only the chimneys on the wings break the symmetry; here, practical considerations outweighed aesthetics. The kitchens required a large, single stack, while Priestley wanted two smaller stacks in his laboratory for the sake of efficiency in performing his experiments.

4 ENTRY HALL

Visitors enter the house today, as they would have in Priestley's time, through the front door, which faces the river, into a large central hallway, where servants or family members would have received guests. Doorways off the hall lead into the drawing room, library, and dining room. A side hallway near the stairs leads to the kitchen area. While the Priestleys lived in the house, the doors off the hall were usually kept closed, for privacy as well as to preserve the heat from their fireplaces, especially in wintertime. Federal-style decorative detailing can be seen in the fanlights over the doors and in the border of dentils, bands of rectangular toothlike blocks, along the top of the walls.

Near the entryway is a plaster statue of Joseph Priestley, a copy of the life-

size statue erected by the city of Birmingham, England, in 1874 on the anniversary of his discovery of oxygen—doubly ironic, since he discovered oxygen before he ever lived in Birmingham, and since it was the Birmingham riots that led him to flee to the United States.

Framed prints from Priestley's era adorn the walls of the hallway and other areas of the house. Although he may not have had these exact images in his house, he would have possessed similar items. All of the original furnishings of the house were sold or passed to his descendants after his death, and no inventory of this house has survived. But in 1791, as part of their claim for compensation from the government for losses from the fire, Priestley and his wife prepared an inventory of their Birmingham house, which lists several portraits, prints, maps, and charts similar to the ones on display in the house today.

5 LIBRARY

Some sixteen hundred books on science, history, and theology once stood on bookshelves lining the walls of Joseph Priestley's library. A large collection for its time, and one of the finest in America, it was especially remarkable considering that he had amassed it in little more than a decade, after the Birmingham riots of 1791 destroyed his library along with an entire lifetime's accumulation of possessions. The books on display in the secretary in this room include both works by him and books he either owned or probably owned.

This room served as Priestley's daily workspace, where he studied, wrote letters and sermons, calculated the results of his experiments, and composed manuscripts for pamphlets and books. After the death of his wife, and especially after he fell ill, Priestley also used this room as his personal apartment, sleeping on a cot placed in the corner where a daybed now stands. In happier times, he and Mary played chess in the evenings, an activity represented by the eighteenth-century chessboard and pieces on display. Mary had done much of the planning for their new home but sadly did not survive to see its completion. Priestley sorely felt her absence, since she had taken care of so many of the details of daily living to free him up for his work. Her portrait above the fireplace is a copy of the original painting at Harris Manchester College, Oxford, which also owns a companion portrait of Mary's husband.

6 LABORATORY

A passageway from the back of the library leads to the laboratory, so that Priestley could easily travel back and forth between his two workspaces. The laboratory was the first section of the house to be finished, in late 1797. Priestley designed the space to suit the specific needs of his experiments. Here, in 1799, he discovered the lethal gas carbon monoxide. In the 1990s, archaeologists uncovered the foundations of two built-in furnaces in the outer corners of the room, to correspond to the two chimneys that once rose from the laboratory wing. Architectural evidence suggests a fume hood, to direct smoke and fumes back out of the house and up the chimneys, was once present. The American Chemical Society donated most of the replica glassware and scientific apparatus on view in the room. Priestley's friend Thomas Cooper acquired much of the original equipment in 1811 when Joseph

Priestley Jr. left the house to return to England. The same year, Cooper moved to Carlisle to become professor of natural philosophy at Dickinson College, which later purchased a number of the items from Cooper. Each year, Dickinson College honors a distinguished scientist with the Priestley Award as a memorial to Dr. Priestley.

7 DRAWING ROOM

In the eighteenth century, the drawing room served as a multipurpose room for family activities, for entertaining guests, and for transacting business such as signing legal documents and settling accounts with local tradesmen and merchants. The Priestleys used the room for two additional, less typical purposes. They held Unitarian services in the room, primarily for fam-

ily members, since there were few other Unitarians in the area. Joseph Priestley also held classes here for young men until the construction of the Northumberland Academy could be completed.

Today, the original drawing room serves primarily as an exhibition space, for displaying artifacts of Priestley family history and the doctor's diverse activities as a scientist, teacher, minister, and author. A fire-damaged iron lock and key on display were among the few items recovered from the ruins of the Priestley house in Birmingham, England. A Wedgwood medallion bust of Priestley is a copy made in 1929 from the original 1773 mold; he had lost

similar medallions of himself, Benjamin Franklin, and others in the Birmingham fire. The oil painting of Franklin above the fireplace is by an anonymous American artist who signed it only as "F. C. C."

Scientific equipment on display includes Priestley's balance scales and the microscope he used to examine plant and animal life in his new American environment. One of his lifelong regrets was that he did not have enough time to become an expert in either botany or zoology.

8 MAIN KITCHEN

A door out of the drawing room leads into the hallway to the kitchen. Four doorways opening along this hallway illustrate the Priestleys' success in combining pragmatic use of space with Georgian aesthetics of symmetry and balance. The door closest to the main hall led to a storeroom for food, cooking equipment, linens, and supplies. The back staircase, for use primarily by servants, rises at the second doorway. The stairs were designed to be narrow enough so that two shallow china or linen closets, fitted with shelves, could be built into the leftover space. This was probably one of the design touches that Joseph Priestley had in mind when he credited his wife with having

"taken much thought in planning the new house," although she did not live to enjoy it.

The kitchen itself looked quite different when the Priestley family lived in the house than it does today. From 1936 to 1955, Penn State leased the property to the Neff family, who owned and operated a hotel in Sunbury. The Neffs served as diligent caretakers of the house; they furnished it with their own private collection of Colonial American antiques and did much to preserve and restore the house itself. They renovated the kitchen in the Colonial Revival style popularized by Colonial Williamsburg, the premier historic preservation effort of the time, and constructed the large single hearth seen in the room today. Colonial American women used hearths like this to cook a variety of dishes simultaneously on several small fires built directly on the hearth floor. But by the 1790s, English families like the Priestleys had cast-iron wood- or coal-burning stoves on which they did most of their cooking. The stove stood within the hearth, making use

of the chimney to carry most of the smoke and fumes out of the house.

The Priestley kitchen also had a second, separate hearth, called a kettle hearth, which kept water hot for household use and could also be used to keep a stockpot simmering with stock used as the base for soups and stews. The Priestleys may have had some of the redware and other early Pennsylvania pottery of the type seen on display in the kitchen today, but they also had Wedgwood and other high-quality china dishes and glasses. Although no inventory survives to tell historians the exact contents of this kitchen, the Birmingham inventory lists 108 pieces of blue-and-white imported "Nankeen china" and a full set of Wedgwood dishes, as well as silver plate and glasses.

The original walls in the kitchen were whitewashed rather than painted as they are today, but the white paint does reflect the color of most

of the house's walls. Studies of two centuries of coats of paint throughout the house revealed that the walls were never wallpapered, which would have been the fashionable choice of the period. The Priestleys had wallpapered rooms in their Birmingham house and in their temporary residence until their new home was finished. Perhaps wallpaper had been Mary

Priestley's preference but her husband decided to forgo the expense after her death.

Doorways in the kitchen lead to the basement and a pantry; neither of these is open to visitors. The door on the street side of the house matches a similar door in the laboratory and thus preserves the Georgian symmetry of the house as seen from the street.

9 BACK KITCHEN

English housewives used their back kitchens for a variety of purposes: laundry, dishwashing, food preparation, light butchering, drying meat and herbs, and perhaps small-scale brewing of cider or ale. The Priestleys' back kitchen took the place of outbuildings found on larger estates of wealthier families, such as a washhouse, brew house, and freestanding kitchen. Archaeological research has revealed

the room's most pragmatic features: a floor that sloped gently to the doorway, so that water could run off naturally and refuse could easily be swept out the door, and a built-in interior well, highly unusual for its time, when most families had outdoor wells. The well is thirty-eight feet deep and tied into the foundation of the room, so it was clearly part of the original construction.

Elizabeth Priestley's work consisted primarily of supervising servants rather than performing all the housework herself, but finding workers in Northumberland was some-times difficult, and she had to do more of the chores herself than she had in England. The Priestleys usually had two maidservants for cooking and cleaning, and a hired man who did gardening and other work. In 1795, they hired a black slave by the week, paying the slaveowner for these services.

10 DINING ROOM

Among genteel families in eighteenth-century England and America, dinner was the main meal of the day. Served as late as two or three o'clock in the afternoon, it usually consisted of several courses and was often a prolonged social occasion for adults in the family. Children ate separately, perhaps with the servants, until they were old enough to participate in adult rituals and discussions. Families ate a late supper at about nine; it was usually cold and often consisted of leftovers from the midday meal.

Most of the furnishings in the house today, such as the dining table, date from the second half of the eighteenth century and are similar to what was in the house when the Priestleys lived there. Like the architecture of the period, Georgian furniture was characteristically simple but elegant. One piece that can be traced directly to Joseph Priestley or his immediate family is the mahogany and brass bracket clock, made by Henry Taylor of London in about 1760.

The portrait of Joseph Priestley over the mantel is a modern one, painted by local artist Beverley Conrad as she imagined him looking in 1794, on his arrival in Northumberland. It resembles a portrait drawn from life by Philadelphia artist Ellen Sharples, probably in Philadelphia in 1794. In both depictions,

Priestley wears a simple black frock coat, without lace or other fashionable accoutrements of the period. After his arrival in America, Priestley followed the style of many American men and gave up wearing a wig, as his friend Benjamin Franklin had done. Unlike all the portraits of Priestley painted in England, these American portraits show him with no wig.

On display inside the built-in glass cabinet on the wall are personal belongings and archaeological fragments, including a piece of porcelain tubing made by Josiah Wedgwood, maker of fine china, who was Priestley's close friend and a fellow member of the Lunar Society in Birmingham. Wedgwood had provided Priestley with free equipment for his experiments in England and continued to send tubing, mortars and pestles, and other apparatus to him in America; in return, Priestley tested Wedgwood porcelain for durability under different temperatures and conditions.

11 STAIRWAY AND UPSTAIRS HALL

In comparison with Great Britain, where land was scarce but labor was plentiful, the American colonies had been land-rich and labor-poor, and this continued to be true in the new nation. Priestley wrote to Benjamin Rush and other friends in Philadelphia begging them to find carpenters willing to come to Northumberland to work on his house. His pleas often went unanswered, and the lack of skilled workmen was the major reason that building the new house was such a time-consuming process. One solution was to purchase some parts of the house ready-made, and this is what Priestley did for his main staircase, which he ordered from Philadelphia. In keeping with the rest of the interior, the staircase is simply but stylishly constructed, without the more extensive ornamentation that was typical in English houses of the period.

The upstairs hallway was not simply a passageway, but

also provided the work and storage space necessary in a house full of people. Living with Joseph Priestley were his eldest son and daughter-in-law and, by 1803, four grandchildren. The family's servants, some of whom may have lived in the house, would have used the back stairs to go to their rooms in the attic; they would have been present on the second floor only when cleaning or performing other duties.

12 **BEDCHAMBER**

The surviving documentation on the house does not indicate where family members slept, except for one brief notation that during his final illness, Dr. Priestley slept in his library. Three bedrooms open onto the second-floor hall; two of these are closed to the public. The remaining

one has been interpreted to represent the bedchamber of Elizabeth Ryland Priestley (1769–1816), the doctor's daughter-in-law who served as mistress of the household.

The PHMC prepared the exhibit in this room in 1995, with the help of a grant from the Pennsylvania Humanities

Council, to represent the domestic space and daily activities of a late-eighteenth-century woman. Of course, she used the room for sleeping, and as was customary, she had fashionable bed curtains. Custom-woven by Sunbury Textile Mills, the fabric, colors, and pattern

are conjectural but replicate common materials of the time.

The woman of the house also used her bedchamber for educating her young children and supervising their play, for sewing and other household tasks that could not be left to servants, and for writing letters. Elizabeth Priestley also wrote three essays for the local newspaper, the *Northumberland Gazette*, defending freedom of thought, speech, and religion—an activity that made her very unusual among women of her day.

1991

University of St. Francis
GEN 324.273 K268 6 ed.
Keefe, William J.
Parties, politics, and public

W9-AEP-504

Parties, Politics, and
Public Policy in America